For Karl
with
[signature]

Incident in Liberation Square
and other poems

Simon Crowcroft

ELSP

Published in 2012 by
ELSP
11 Regents Place
Bradford on Avon
Wiltshire BA15 1ED
www.ex-librisbooks.co.uk

Origination by Seaflower Books
Typeset in 11pt Times New Roman

Printed by CPI Group (UK) Ltd,
Croydon, CR0 4YY

ISBN 978-1-906641-45-0

© 2012 Simon Crowcroft

For G.K. Crowcroft

Acknowledgements

Some of these poems have previously appeared in *Wavelengths: New poetry in the Channel Islands*, the *Jersey Evening Post*, and the Bridport Prize anthology. 'Coup' was first broadcast on BBC Radio 3.

Contents

Incident in Liberation Square	9
Compulsory showers	10
In woods near Brize Norton	11
The American military cemetery, Cambridge	12
At Omaha	13
En route to Pegasus Bridge	14
After the 2nd XI beat St Catharine's	15
Buying lemons	16
In memory of Richard Marsh, drowned on naval exercises	17
This new face	18
The middle son	19
Now this ring	20
Horse chestnuts	21
The magic town	22
Rose clouds in the bare windows	24
To a lover who admits to a belief in reincarnation	25
Age difference	26
The imprisoned God	29
Autobiography	28
In memory of Gerard Le Claire	29
Talismans	30
The artist and his dog in the River Ystwyth	32
The indirect approach	33
The sticker protocol	34
From *Mean Streets* (1994)	
By-pass	36
Beware the minotaur	37
For all their pains	38
As I was walking down Mulcaster Street	40
Mean streets	42

An occupation	43
Evidence	44
Crutches	45

From *A Texan Urn* (2003)

Coup	48
And the purpose of your visit?	49
Leibfraumilch	50
Gazebo	52
Nature's failures	53
This old man	54
Cigar	56
A Texan urn	57
In Houston airport chapel	57
Words on blue	60
Email	61
Savings	62
Looking	63
Caught mid-sentence in an empty room	64
The visit	65
Look-alike	66
Driving lessons	67
August	68
Exeats	69
Below Wytham	70

Incident in Liberation Square

Thierry's the one with the wide smile, perfect teeth
and diseased heart, who leaves his books on his desk
(A*dvanced Learner's Dictionary, A Modern Grammar,
Cambridge English for Holiday Courses*)

not because he's idle but to avoid their combined weight
on the short walk back, where the host-family I selected
pampers him with low-fat, low-salt, low-sugar meals
and a complete absence of stairs.

We handle him like a single long-stemmed glass
among tumblers, would bubble-wrap him, or place staff
on all sides like police outriders, but to his peers,
forgetful of Monday's briefing, he's just a student:

they jostle past him in the corridor, muss his hair,
land soft punches on his shoulder; when he comes to the office
to quiz me about the zoo trip, there's a Polish girl
on each side, their arms draped lovingly around his neck.

He likes it here – likes the sea, where he floats,
grinning back at the sun, or goes gingerly into the surf;
likes the young German who offers him her towel,
eyeing his scars, a top Parisian surgeon's handiwork;

likes our Liberation Square, where on Friday he walks
with the girls, talks in four languages, and is assaulted:
head-butted, kicked in the face, the ribs, the groin;
'French scum!' my compatriots call him, kicking on.

Compulsory showers

The boy and the girl in the naked crowd
knew each other from swimming classes.
Once, frog-kicking past each other slowly,
(he had not mastered the crawl like his bronzed peers)
her instep was swept by his heel, and he apologised;
they had sat by the pool-side: she wanted
to play in an orchestra; he would become a doctor.

True, they had day-dreamed, he more than she:
the baring of her breasts, the colour of her bush – it *was* black,
but her shaven head was not in his scheme of things;
his hair had always been short, but for a girl
whose fancy dared go no further than a kiss,
it was a shock to see his genitals.

Luckily the male queue flowed faster:
he saw a boy with a crimson face
trying to hide his erection;
she saw the divided husbands
and wives, exchanging encouraging words,
twisting bright rings in their grooves.

In woods near Brize Norton

The squirrels have reached the end of their cachés,
they pause between the vast tree boles,
frisk their tails,
scratch at last year's leaf fall,
taking pot luck like gold-diggers.

The grey planes rise overhead,
like tall leaping horses
whose riders tug on metal reins
trampling the woods with hooves of noise.

This the squirrels are used to,
they dig on like beavers;
it is my helpless raising of my hands
to plug my ears
that startles them up the trees.

The American military cemetery, Cambridge

If they had less than their share of years
these dead visitors can at least take pride
in their allotment up here above Madingley;
when our names are reallocated,
our untended graves requisitioned for gardens,
these few thousand will continue to be.

America gave the best dollars could buy,
each cross carved better than the last
in starch-white Portland stone,
well-placed trees of beech, catalpa, pagoda,
an invisible host of groundsmen
to clip the exact box hedges and lawn.

Surveying such magic, a superintendent
grows old here, distributes his fact sheet
(the flagpole's height, the depth of the oblong pools),
expatiates in the chapel, an Ops. room
mapping the war's progress, while overhead
mosaic squadrons enter heaven with the angels.

At Omaha

The Impressionists at Vierville-sur-Mer
would have painted such a scene: the dark bluff
of Pointe-du-Hoc, the wide sands firm enough
for horse-riding, a striped deck-chair,
a fishing boat breasting the mounting swells,
a glimpse of your back as you stoop for shells.

Like sentries, local authority signs
defend the hill: one must not play
loud music, litter, pick flowers, or stray
from the path on protected dunes;
our bare feet drum the boardwalk through the reeds,
fat bees hum in lillies, and cottony seeds

drift out of the willows, clogging the brook
as they have always done in June.
Banks of daisy, speedwell and celandine
make way for lawns, and a black look
from the cemetery warden, who knows
from our sandy feet, where I plucked your wild rose.

En route to Pegasus Bridge

for Clive Kemp

Pass in comfort over drowned meadows,
doomed intersections, the fatal hill;
nothing remains, yet from the windows
glimpses tease your memory: the spill
of hay from broken barns, the hedgerows
thick with may, the spire at Bénouville.

Plant the wooden cross in Dransfield's grave,
who took your place in the turret, and
bullets meant for you. Bless him who gave
long nights and days by the ten thousand,
and asked for nothing in return, save
this 'Thank you', in a spidery hand.

After the 2nd XI beat St Catharine's

Heberden's dead
drowned in his own bed
should have lined his stomach
with milk and bread.

Sober next door
I slept better than ever before
the din of his hi fi like tom toms
resounding no more.

As the trivial act
proves of most consequence
so Heberden stirred
and lay on his back,

the knees of his cricket whites
green from his last catch
and red on his thigh
from his first maiden.

Buying lemons

Their goods swathed in polythene,
traders lurk in dim shelters, the stall of fruit
and flowers the only one where a queue grows.

Day-glo men with hammers and crow-bars
batter a grate in a foaming gutter;
it stays fast for all their pains.

Lemons from a hot Sicilian grove
where an adder basks in a broken wall
and twigs crackle in the heat.

Buses sail the wet streets
with bow waves and wakes of spray
bound for the long low Cambridge suburbs.

On the dark stairs the lemons burst the wet bag,
bounce high and skew to the door and the lawn
where daffodils bloom and magnolia buds.

Richard impales one on his umbrella –
he's back from a sortie for spices,
his blazer dry as a bone, his Diana laughing.

In memory of Richard Marsh, drowned on naval exercises

Richard, recipient of my longest epistles,
this is a letter you won't have to read;
remember I tried to convert you,
to give you the password you didn't need?

Under a smoke-screen to hide us from Finals
you argued with me about God, your talk
ship-shape for Dartmouth,
your gait more a march than a walk.

You knew where you were going, you said,
your blue eyes fixed on the horizon,
scanned from the bridge of your first command,
your fair hair clipped for a career in the sun.

Yet you were, drawn, weren't you, when you met
the Christians in their joy, Bible-handed, off somewhere
or heard the singing in an upper room and found,
later, in the bar, their looks too bright to bear?

Look at me now, confused, apostate,
your being, apparently, in hell, added to my wrongs;
did I fail you? Tell me, what were your dumb cries
as you drank the sea to slake your burning lungs?

This new face

I need practice wearing this new face the windows
tell me is mine, the follicles abandoned like rows
of trenches; beggared by the rich heads of girls
I foresee how the years will scythe my sons' curls,
extending their foreheads to their crowns,
the shared comb's cardings in our drains.

This is my inheritance, with incisors
whose neat mating the dentist admires,
from my shadowy but balding ancestors,
their bare pates shining in the light of their fires.

The middle son

The middle son
wreathed in his mother's scent
waved until the train had gone.

Too young to care, too old,
his brothers raced to the 'Travellers Fare' –
the middle son

sure it was something he had done,
his messy room, his noisy play,
waved until the train had gone.

His father standing there
recalled the sudden smart of beard,
the middle son

half-asleep, reaching out
to a parent gone by morning, and his son
waved until the train had gone.

'It won't be long', he said –
he lied, he was still waiting;
the middle son
waved until the train had gone.

Now this ring

Now this ring has escaped oblivion
as removed for rough work on a garden pot
it was not taken by magpies or lost to the worms,
consigned to a pocket for days it outsmarted
the faulty seam, missed gratings by inches,
retrieved from cloakrooms, the workshop's woodshavings,
survived abrasion, the atoms of gold dropped
wherever I went, the burglar's ransacking
and the ring-stripping cold of the sea;
it has won safe-keeping, slipped from the hand,
(suddenly naked and afraid) and discarded
in a drawer with souvenirs and foreign coins.

Horse chestnuts

Under horse chestnuts a concert with bees,
the ground bass, the noise of the leaves
like an audience rustling programmes, a dove
coos – you, you, I love, I love you, I love –
breaking off to give the rabble of songbirds
their turn, and the gulls flying seawards.

Listen, the bird is calling and getting
faint answers from the distance, sending
an urgent code along the avenue –
love, love, I love you, I love you –
in the green shade hung with magic lanterns
there's applause from the leaves. It sidesteps, turns

cocks its small grey head, its bright beady eyes
watching the tops of passing cars, the flies
crawling on the leaves, this figure below
looking up, making no noise. Or does he blow
through cupped hands – I, I love you, I –
waiting for a reply?

The magic town

Your husband wanted a quick sale,
waved the sign at the street like a flag
of surrender, tempered your distress
with a visit to a northern town
comforted by hills, where property's cheaper,
and the promise of your own car.
After you went the lights burned so late
I abandoned my vigil, it was so clearly
not you behind the makeshift curtains;
you always went up early, to your husband's chagrin,
makers of spells needing their sleep, or time
in their books, away from the television.

Perhaps they were all charmed,
the circle of your friends who found
gifts bestowed on them each time they called,
or was I the only one whose hand
received a light caress in taking hold
of my portion in what you had no use for?
They've lost their properties now, just things,
there's nothing here that wears your scent,
or conjures up images. I could rub
their surfaces for hours, no spirit in your guise
would appear to me, offering favours.

Your house has cast off its aurora
yet your magical effects linger
around the town, its least bright quarters
invested with special status by our walks,
our rendezvous. And though it's true

I shall never meet you in the streets,
or accompany you home across the park,
the town holds your warmth like a stone,
and I can imagine, centuries on,
archeological surveys will find
traces of our emotion here, like barrows.

Rose clouds in the bare windows

Rose clouds in the bare windows –
it took a clock to wake us,
lost among the crumpled pillows,
our bearings slowly found with kisses.

What could come between me and you,
laced by fingers, arms and thighs
but a golden hair you softly drew
out from our mouths? Nothing in your eyes

prepared me for this, the second's grace
when sparrows wake me, the tears that run
along the contours of the face
down routes they took at twelve and one.

And so it will be until I find
they have dissolved at every hour
each treaty of love we wrote and signed,
so true, so sure, all twenty four.

To a lover who admits to a belief in reincarnation

Older than your father whose déjà vu
told you he started out a wimpled nun,
you show me in your present apparition
galleries of self-portraits. Who are you,
and how can you expect your love to not
ridicule this leap-frogging of the grave,
from ruffian jabbering in his cave
through bird and beetle back to the year dot?

Put your borrowed arms round me, I won't mock
your creed, despite the séance tape you played
on which you drown, and the rape of a maid
in medieval times; it's poppycock,
of course, this strange affiliation to the dead,
the provisional way you smile and nod your head.

Age difference

See how the world was before you were born:
the topsy-turvy southern hemisphere,
winter barbecues, the tree on the lawn,
bright with baubles. What was I doing there
but kicking my heels in our rented home,
as your parents converged in other lands?
My problem wasn't middle-child syndrome
but the four winds showing their empty hands.
Then your parents conjoined in cross-section,
their intimate embrace on public view
in the book left out for my attention,
(not just any old blastocyst, but you!)
and a new star blazed away in the north,
baffling astronomers as I set forth.

The imprisoned God

The imprisoned God wears flagstones thin
on his calloused immortal knees,
but answering the prayers of the faithful
keeps his spirits up. Needing no food or drink
he runs up no bills, and the space is vacant, anyway.
Does he note the jingle of receding keys?
(He could snap the bars of this ageing heart
with his little finger.)

Sometimes when my mind is quiet
I hear him singing the anthems he taught me:
'Be valiant, be strong, resist the pow'r of sin!'
that sort of stuff. He doesn't think I hear;
he sings to himself, the way I used to,
when I was his grateful prisoner.

Some mornings on the coast road, queuing in traffic,
I wind the window down, and watch the furling waves,
and listen to the surf and seabirds' cries,
and sing with him.

Autobiography

I used to pretend, used to walk up
the kerb as a tightrope, as a child,
like Blondin, arms out, over the drop;
child's play to some, stiffened and old,
watching my sandalled foot slip
and me trying again, as if I could.

I had luck, sprung in a safe land,
favoured by parents, kings and climate;
my faults were never fatal – the second
early or late, the foot too short,
too far – I escaped the breath of wind
with its germ, the bullets, the meteorite.

The tightrope I didn't see, how it
swung with the weight of the others,
but heard people falling, their sad shout
and the gasp of spectators;
I was pressed along on slippery feet,
the blindfold wet with my tears.

In memory of Gerard Le Claire

He tried so hard to look older:
glasses, goatee, gruelling missions
to the world's end on shoestring budgets;
fresh-faced for all his pains, as if some shaman
had slipped him an elixir, at lectures
they would think a schoolboy had come to the dais.
Imagine him at sixty, walking the shoreline
between South Hill and the Dicq,
with crows' feet, at last, and his hair silver!

Loving this place, he loved the world more –
'The local is global' – et cetera:
rivers in the wrong places,
downpours drumming on the sea,
the earth crazed like old china …

'We must meet up for a beer,' he'd say,
pumping my hand, and we had years to arrange it:
this table with its view of the sea,
a cargo ship crossing St Aubin's Bay,
and two glasses, one empty, the other full.

Talismans

At weekends Dad pushed the mess to the landings;
by Thursday it lapped over every flat surface,
stairways narrowing to precarious passes, stuff
teetering on the piano top, Sunday's table settings
glimpsed between laundry piled up like vraic: unused
dessert forks, the Haywain's underwater dog,
scraps of the roast like biltong.

Virgin birth wasn't our christmas miracle
but Dad's transformation of the house while Mum
was out shopping. 'Where'd it all go?' she'd cry,
turning sideways to come through the door
with all her bags, her pleasure at the sudden light
and space checked by a sense of things gone for good.

She'd keep a till receipt for twenty years
if I let her. Lately she's been producing granny's clothes,
which reek of camphor, 'They'll fit you perfectly now',
she says, sizing them up to me. My babygrows
are stored somewhere – what kind of hint is that?

Things Dad couldn't chuck he put in attic boxes
always meaning to sort: a wooden train he'd fix,
'No trouble, just needs a drop of glue'; a china cup
he smashed with a champagne cork; bits of plastic
from a complex toy we never assembled, the one chance
passing before the instructions were thrown away.

Its yellow rods, blue sprockets, grey cogs, still turn up
when I spring clean, or helping in the garden,
turn over the rich loam for my Mum,
and the pieces will sit in my pocket for days
before I can bring myself to throw them away.

The artist and his dog in the River Ystwyth

Jack leaps from the path into the gorge,
crosses the oxbow pool and finds his red frisbee.
It's no sooner at his master's feet than Clive
flings it out again, only this time it falls short
and he must strip to his boxers and jump,
yelping at the cold, protesting he can't afford
to waste another six quid on his dog.

'Butterfingers!' he yells as we miss the catch
and it bounces back into deep water;
Peter, worried about Clive's heart,
explains the error of the Victorians,
removing meanders to save on bridges,
but the river in spate – he points out the flotsam
above our heads – carried off the silver rails.

Blue with cold, Clive vies for our attention,
wet Jack his brush, the stone beach his canvas.

The indirect approach

Alone in the gents he grunts to himself:
'Patience, old cock, patience! Splashing his face
under the tap, his eyes hiss like hot coals.

He has controlled his use of the f-word,
his instinct to slit her throat when caught out –
'Vote?' he'd scoffed. Her hazel eyes had narrowed.

The mirror tautens at his grimaces.
She's paid the bill by the time he returns –
she's his for the price of a few roses.

The sticker protocol

Aged ten, her favourite grandson displays
a flair for antiques. From her Parker Knoll
(bagged by her eldest in '72) Grandma says

he must place a sticker next to, not over,
all prior requests: the clock on the wall
is promised to his mum; his dad, lover

of pink lustre china, has stickered those;
behind the upright piano, a rival
has staked a claim in faded turquoise.

He puts his name in a set of Dickens;
the varnished globe in its walnut gimbal,
with so much empire-red, turns

as he tilts its base; he leaves 'A Vision
of the Last Judgement,' askew in the hall,
Grandpa's sticker replaced with his own.

From *Mean Streets* (1994)

By-pass

The roadmaker's craft lies also in the signs
screening paved meadows, divided farms,
as if a crow had flown
straight across the land I knew,
these level acres its wide black wake.

The forest I never understood is ash;
it's clear now how the village stands
in relation to the town,
why long circuitous walks were unnecessary
down the undulating road few used.

No quantity of faith moved these hills;
certain nomads encamped here,
tethered their beasts in this dust-bowl
and went, the scars grassing over,
to cut their way through another shire.

Beware the minotaur

What wide inhuman maw?
What needless sacrifice?
What paralysing roar?

The rubbish people talk!
You won't be eaten –
Just look both ways and walk.

Armed with the Green Cross Code
More young islanders
Brave the mouth of the road.

For Ariadne's thread
Has rotted in the dark
And Theseus is dead.

For all their pains

For all their pains: the clear-headed sperm,
the abstemious ovum, the infant who swam
in sober seas (till she was full-term
he renounced lunchtime beer and the wee dram

at bedtime); for all the sterile rooms
and hospital gowns, each ante-natal session,
the earnest men with ears to wombs
like eavesdroppers; the sudden conversion

to home-birth, the doctor's dark word
of disaster (the flying squad trapped
in traffic, the child hanged by the cord);
for the kitchen like a library, the mother rapt

in Leboyer and Kitzinger; winning the fight,
for the birth in their bed, the father asleep
at his post, the midwife arriving at first light
with the milk-float; for all the hours without sleep,

the checking and re-checking of the cot,
kept awake by the hi-tech gismo, hearing
each catch in his breathing, checking he had not
turned on his front, always checking and fearing;

for all of the warm clothes washed and dried,
the coats, straps, and clips, done, undone,
every door locked, buckle-restraint tied,
for every precaution and vaccination;

for all the kerbside drills, the lessons
in fear, the child chauffeured here, there
and everywhere, the tireless explanations,
(You cannot walk – just think of the danger!)

for all their pains, came a killing machine,
someone in a hurry, or an alcoholic haze,
and for the child out for sweets, or a magazine,
called a visitor early by ten thousand days.

As I was walking down Mulcaster Street

As I was walking down Mulcaster Street
An old man took me by the arm;
'Now you be fit,' he said, 'and you be fleet,
Help me cross so I meet no harm.'

'So I meet no harm as my neighbour did
On the ring road in St Saviour,
He saw the bright stars when he heard the van skid,
He went up to meet his Maker.'

'You should use the crossing, good sir,' I said,
'You may go across in safety,
Press the button and when the lights turn red,
you may go across in safety.'

'Cross in safety, my hat!' he said, 'Oh where
Is the pedestrian crossing?'
I looked up the street, and I looked down, there
Was no pedestrian crossing.

'Then you must wait until the traffic slows
To arrive at the bus station,
One of these rushing drivers surely knows
You walk to a destination.'

'Shall I wait until the loud crack of doom?'
He called out as I was leaving;
He stepped into the street, into his tomb,
And all his friends are grieving.

Then a man from Public Services came,
He set up a ticking meter,
Said, 'By my yellow coat, we aren't to blame,
The old man should have been fleeter.'

Mean streets

Public Services do not care –
their holes in the ground, the ash in their hair
their main concerns, and traffic flow,
not the mean streets where pedestrians go.

Tourism moguls do not care –
they let the hapless tourist dare
our gridlocked roads, and advertise
Jersey: a walker's paradise.

Parents of small children care –
there's a guard on the fire, a gate on the stair
but nowhere to cross from the house to the shops,
their street a racetrack that never stops.

Eager commuters do not care –
they hardly see the pedestrian there,
but other cars, of course, let pass
with a nod or a wave through tinted glass.

Politicians do not care –
they like to park in the Royal Square,
"If we make the bankers commute by bus
they're hardly going to vote for us!"

Workers in the hospital care –
confronted by the injured there;
and nurses cool, calm surgeons, porters whistling tunes
dread morning's harvest and the afternoon's.

An occupation

No muffled anchor chain dropping in the bay,
and queasy soldiers disembarked by night,
or bullets from the blue sky splintering
wood and bone, and flagrant foreign flag –

We thought these were our friends! Not threatening
but gracious, arriving in ones and twos,
finding favour with the natives, and when
their ships had doors, and they crowded ashore,

Welcome! we said. Then reinforcements came,
tankers with supplies, teams of engineers
who changed the land, the laws. Who could refuse
orders like theirs? For least resistance meant

in some houses silent rooms, in some schools
chairs tucked under desks all day. And watching
their manoeuvres now, their constant convoys
drawn across our paths, we are afraid.

Leashed to our sides our children see no gleam
of an insurgent's eye in our craven stares;
only late at night when the patrols slacken
we stroll across the avenue to the sands.

Evidence

Like any Friday, turning out
his pockets, the crumpled cards,
the pencil stub, the balloon shards,
the sticky sweets, the stale crust –
hard facts in a world of doubt,
where everything turns to dust.

The seams still intact,
resewn to the fly
from the crotch and thigh,
but the right leg needs attention,
holed by the car's impact
and the road's abrasion.

And the knee patches like muslin –
'What do you get up to at school,
for godsake! Do you
work on your knees?'
His trousers kick and run
under the trees.

Crutches

Remember the first yards across the ward's
miles of polished lino, crutches akimbo,
and silvered in the slanting sun,
the exercise as impossible
as crossing a falls?

Then some expert would swing by,
I'd say, 'You'll be like that, pretty soon' –
'Never!' you'd scowl,
flinging the crutches down,
getting your burning leg horizontal.

And the sweating physiotherapist -
remember how he kept leaving off
your torture to mop his face,
how the pools of his perspiration
impeded your progress?

Like overdue books, for months
they were left in the hall, save when
you machine-gunned your brothers with them,
or took trips around the uneven yard
for old times' sake.

From *A Texan Urn* (2003)

Coup

He's dead, I heard at breakfast; by lunchtime
the present tenses had been rounded up and shot;
I couldn't say at dusk, my father works abroad,
owes me a letter, or that he does anything.
The future tenses, his 'wills', his 'going to's', have fled
dropping promises behind them, and in the squares
the second person pronoun wars against the third,
addressing the dead as if alive, as if listening,
at last, to my language – 'I love you'
scrawled like graffiti in the occupied streets.
For the past holds the town, it always did:
he taught me to keep still when watching animals;
he used to pull back my shoulders to correct
this stoop; he left home when I was ten.

And the purpose of your visit?

And the purpose of your visit?
To show myself how easy it is
(six identical hostesses leaving
by another door beat this queue)
how I could have come each year,
on the new jets, an old hand at picking
the quickest line through immigration,
with hand luggage only, the year's news,
and thirty visas in pastel colours.

My passport creaks with disuse,
its single stamp from several years back,
its photo of the bearer as a younger man.
I need not say a word. Marshalled here,
between 'for business' and 'for pleasure'
the bereaved stand out a mile.
Thank you, Sir. Enjoy your visit.

Leibfraumilch

This grateful alumnus says my father changed his life.
Bill - bright eyes, checked shirt, energetic step –
pumps my hand. 'Who's gonna cut the cakes?'
the widow cries. We sit around the pastries,
Bill bends forward, takes the knife and serves me first.
'Thanks'.
'You bet.'
'Yessir, his classes were ... (Thank you, You bet)
inspiring, it wasn't like work, you forgot where you were ...
(Some for you, M'am?) A colleague of my father's
accepts a slice. 'He was a mine of information,
you could ask him anything under the sun
and what he didn't know right there and then
he'd go and find out.'

The widow repeats the one about the time he'd taken
with an anxious candidate who'd telephoned late –
'But Peter, it's three in the morning! Honestly!'
the same reproachful squeal, the same reaction,
heads nodding with reverence, or shaking with awe.
We eat the cakes and drink Leibfraumilch,
'his favourite, you know.' I didn't,
I had no idea my father liked sweet white wine.

They bring me their tributes, these alumni,
these colleagues of my dad, their gratitude
for his prodigality with words. I say,
'For me his voice was just a memory
even when he was alive'.

The widow sips her wine. The awkward silence
Bill breaks at last with a slow uncomprehending nod,
a breath drawn in between his teeth, a meditative
'Hey.'

Gazebo

The widow brings the funeral left-overs and withdraws.
In the gazebo her son blames his father's death
on DIY, the summerhouse floor laid brick by brick,
this fancy seat he never stopped to rest on.
'Jesus, could he swear! If he banged his thumb
we went out for a taco while he chilled out.'

Do I remember his temper?
Hardly. A smack before dawn on a birthday
for unwrapping the present too soon, brown paper
crackling like wood fire.

                                        Hammer-welts here
where he belaboured the pine, punishing the skewed nail,
the cracked timber, the nagging pain in his back.
His hammer still lifts and falls, rings in the distance
with his curses, damning himself a senile bloody fool,
a stupid bloody cack-handed old man.

The structure wants priming before the flattened nail heads,
most of them evenly-spaced and true, start to rust.

Nature's failures

Driven to work now, he bends his knees and lies flat.
He tries to guess the route between his home
and the university, from upper windows, the wires
looping between poles, and birds crossing an unfinished skyline.
His wife-cum-nurse-cum-chauffeur has put her hair in a bun
as she always does when she's angry. His colleagues, half his age,
are on vacation, supine on Florida's beaches or the Bahamas,
but he must teach as if there's no tomorrow, though it took an hour
to get him up and dressed. She'd be madder if she knew
he's been popping pills like a junkie since break of day.

'And this guy's supposed to knock 'em dead with his classes?
He's late, he mumbles.' The student at the back
his sneakers squeaking on the seat in front
looks round for support, reverses his cap, gets out a paper
to check the Longhorns' form against the Chicago Bulls.

The old lecturer has shuffled as far as the dais but cannot climb
the three steps. He's like a mechanical toy on its last wind.
Some girls in the front row help him to the lectern which he grips
as if it's a zimmer frame. Switching on the mike he thanks
the girls graciously with a quip that makes the hall laugh
and the girls blush. 'Today's lecture is Nature's failures,' he begins.
He looks up, and the next laugh turns all heads to the back,
where the boy, his face crimson, has folded his newspaper
and put his feet down.

This old man

In South Austin Hospital
invoices hang at the end of the beds,
the nurses have accountants' hands,
switching off the patients' bells
to concentrate on ledgers; gowning up
the surgeon hears a mobile phone
ring under the pinstripe. 'The garage wants to know ...'
The only mistakes that matter here
are clerical, a wrong decimal point,
a syringe not charged for.

                    This old man
has a hole in his back where
doctors have prospected for marrow,
a bandage no one will remember to change.

After Friday's chemotherapy
he's parked on the wrong floor with hip replacements:
urged to keep upright (on his powder spine)
he troops gamely down with the others
to the gloom of the basement pool
where horizontal in the shallows he watches
one who flounders as if learning to swim,
another whom a nurse is absent-mindedly drowning,
not hearing for all the laughter and splashing
the sound of oars across the black water –
the boatman is coming for him.

Retrieved by the right ward (they thought him dead already)
he fills the ward with his wisecracks
as if emanating good cheer from a hospital bed
had been his life's goal, he gives a last lesson there,
counting for the benefit of some contract nurses
the billions of bacteria at work on him.

Morning brings his young wife with fresh flowers;
the pastor renews his advances, though for her
a different kind of benediction stirs.

Cigar

We lunch at a restaurant overlooking the river.
There's a couple he worked for in his spare time
(what spare time?) as a tutor in their private college.
Having revered him they wanted to meet his son,
they said. They're insisting I stop by their college to meet
some of the students who loved my father so much.
I won't go.

Over the meal's babble, the clink of silver, china, glass,
comes the sound of rowers, the united dip of oars
at each strong stroke, and the coxswain's commands.

On the balcony a man and a woman are watching,
sharing an enormous cigar. When I first saw it passed,
I thought, this woman in the red dress is just tasting it,
but now it seems she is smoking more of it than he is.
Maybe it's her cigar. There is cheering on the river.
They smile at each other in the sun.

I have been discussing American and British beers
with the manager: these half-dozen bottles
held different brews I have sampled 'on the house'.
They make a useful barricade.

The couple who have come to reminisce
about my late father must be disappointed:
no "customary suits of inky black" here,
just a drunk ogling some woman across the restaurant.

A Texan urn

Today I stood in his office cleared of everything
but a yellow post-it note on the filing cabinet:
'Back at 2.30 – P.C.' and the next lecturer's effects,
boxed, awaiting the start of the fall semester.

From the window level with the crowns of limes
I watched the squirrels on the lawns and the blue jays,
my hand on the sill beating time as his did perhaps,
waiting for a late student to show.

'Did I show you the ashes yet?' I'm asked while packing –
'They're just next door.' I say, 'I think I'll pass on the ashes.'
This must seem worse than my refusal to enjoy Texas,
(the Alamo was offered, and downtown Austin)

and I wonder, because I have not felt his dead weight
or realised how much of him was vapour,
will I find myself looking forward to the next letter,
the next visit? Should I go next door and find

a Texan urn, mass-produced in plastic,
embellished with laurel wreaths or neo-classic forms
and will the ubiquitous steer
still rear its horns in imitation mahogany?

Leaving for the airport at dawn, I see him walking away:
he is thinking of the next projects in house and garden;
he crosses the footbridge, enters the park, where the hobos
are stirring on the benches, stretching and stamping,

sharing the first drink of the day. 'Hiya Doc,'
they greet him. He grins and swaps the briefcase
of students' work to the other hand.
A leaf falls: there's a whole lecture there.

In Houston airport chapel

'All welcome.' Anything goes
in the airport's ecumenical chapel.
No clock times the dim lights' perpetual dusk,
the indeterminate blue-green decor,
and pictureless, windowless walls offend none.
Empty of travellers and of meanings, it is at least
a quiet place to sit, away from security announcements,
the carpet clean enough for prayer mats
or for my back exercises, come to think of it.

A Bible has been sneaked in and left open
at Psalm 15: 'Lord, who shall dwell in thy tabernacle?'
That's the million dollar question, that is.

In transit in Houston did he dart in here
to save a dollar from the shoeshine?
I put his name in the visitors book, and, 'R.I.P'.
Other people's comments are more original:
'Wife missing for two days – please pray'.
'May the Lord have mercy on our baggage'.
'Zach, you were great last night,
meet me here again tomorrow – Steve.'

Faint muzak beckons from the departures hall,
and bagels, pastries, donuts, pizza, fries.

Words on blue

Amongst his boxes of correspondence
I found my letters, every one.
What I was looking for were his last words,
"By the time you read this, my son ..."

Advice would be in keeping; a secret
he always wanted me to share;
philosophy, in closing; a p.s.,
"At last, you owe me a letter!"

I brought all of his letters to Texas
and am bringing all of my letters back,
the epistolary history of my life
no substitute for what I lack.

Collated on the long flight home, at last
the aerogrammes are in sequence;
the monologue starts now the dialogue's done
and after that will come silence.

This is all that there was, these messages
across oceans, these words on blue;
Why did you leave them for me to find?
These were yours for keeps; they were for you.

Email

*(A former colleague of his writes: "I would be happy
to correspond with you about your late father, though
I doubt the internet is an appropriate medium.")*

Printed out, screwed into a ball, this grudging email
lands in the bin with a "Fuck you, then". Later on
I can explain: there we were, finally, gifted

with the means to communicate instantly and almost
for free, our words transcending ink and paper,
the dust of a dozen depots, the cold of the hold

high over the Atlantic, and the need to reply
to forgotten questions or bother with old news.
But he only said, "I cannot get used to email,

there is a kind of indecent haste transmitting
personal notes by electrons!" Day after day,
we booted up our respective computers,

and sorted through the messages from strangers,
deleting the junk mail and offers to get rich quick,
or reading them, I suppose, if we had time on our hands.

Savings

What if that decade of intercessions was not wasted,
after all, and amongst the thoughts launched skywards
prayers for my father's salvation were deposited?

Wouldn't there be due a pay-out, bigger than a cold-cure,
or coincidence, or benefit that might have accrued anyway –
a top-of-the-range sign, unambiguous as stigmata?

So, driving down through Illinois, a licence-plate in front
(catching the sun) read, 'GOD IS', and that night,
asleep in his motel room he had a dream - 'orgasmic',

he wrote, with customary frankness – that God was true,
and now it was his turn to pray for me. But if he did,
the transactions were made in another currency,

for from behind the pane of misted glass
the teller breaks the silence of a lifetime:
'Your account with us is closed.'

Looking

You had no idea that you were looking at him
for the last time; your bad back making you hobble
like an older man, while he was light on his dancer's feet,
swinging his bag which you had tried to carry for him,
but had given up without a struggle.

You watched him queue behind many panes of glass
not turning, expecting that you had left him
as he had left you, his old curiosity at work
inspecting his boarding card, then the people around him,
finding interest in the prosaic.

You saw his arms go up at security,
and for a moment he was like a hostage,
or someone trying to surrender in a hail of fire –
you may have wondered then if you would see him again,
stepping up to the glass to be seen.

You saw him smile at the official
as he was frisked, and something he said to the stranger –
you imagined the sort of remark –
made all around him laugh, before he turned,
passing briskly through the door.

Caught mid-sentence in an empty room

Caught mid-sentence in an empty room –
'Who are you talking to, Dad?' he asks.
In his godless stable world, father is a word
the posh use, so I say I was talking to my Dad.

Fathers believe the boarding-school brochures,
consign their children to incompetent care
and the company of the brutal; Dads
are accessible after school, though they may hide
in the garage or at the computer. Fathers
put oceans in the way; dads are just there.

He complains that I am here, talking to myself,
instead of talking to him about homework
or whatever it was that brought him up here.
He's right. We'll go downstairs together.

The visit

I dreamed my father wandered into my room
while I was writing. He was looking for a book
he said, he'd not read for years and now was not likely to.

The shelves are double-stacked. I used to buy boxloads
before a simple sum proved I had too many to read,
even if I outlived him. "That Steinbeck looks familiar.

Yep. It's mine." He takes another book from the shelf.
"This any good?" "Dunno. I haven't read many of my books.
I just keep reading the same old things – Hardy, Lawrence."

"I can't stand either of them," he says. He peers at the screen:
"Shouldn't waste so much time hunched over that thing."
The smell of his clothes and beard reaches me.

I want to show him the memorial I've put on the internet:
his picture, obituary, excerpts from his unfinished book,
but can't get the computer to log on. When he's gone

I'll connect easily, no doubt. "Keep that back straight,"
he says from the doorway, then, "Bye, boy." Kind, forgetful,
his parting words, with all the pills, like gravel.

Look-alike

From a distance the old man with the dog
resembles my father, though he never owned a dog
or cat. What would a zoologist want with a dog
when he got home? But when we lived in Australia
he kept wombats, and anyone walking towards me
with a wombat would remind me of those days
as surely as this man does, who says 'Heel' to his dog
as we pass; but who, despite the pepper-and-salt goatee
and mottled hands, has neither laughter in his eyes,
nor any shadows gathering on his brow.

Driving lessons

'Step on the gas, or you'll cause an accident,'
he snaps. I am driving my father across town
on his last visit – I am driving my father mad
with this snail's pace, slowing for people to cross,
the way I do since my son was knocked down.

There's a horn blast behind but I hit the brakes:
a woman with more kids than she can hold onto
smiles at me as she leads them across, and at the old man
beside me pulling his cloth cap over his eyes with a frown.

'How long have we been bipeds?' I ask him.
'Six million years. But folk still had to watch their step
when there were dinosaurs about.' He knows I know
that's anachronistic. He sneaks a look at the burgeoning queue.
'Jesus God!' he mutters. 'Did I teach you to drive?'

'Studies show,' I say, appealing to the scientist in him,
'communities severed by busy roads grow whole again
when traffic slows like this. People make friends
across the street, take more exercise ...'
But he has put his head in his hands.
'Thank Christ no one knows me round here,' he groans.

His hands are smaller than I remember them,
teaching me to drive, grabbing the wheel of his rented car
when I veered into playing fields or towards the river.
That black mark on the back of his neck
his doctor has pronounced benign. In front of us
a man his age nods a thank you, and crosses sprightly.

August

August ages his image a year:
it thins the face, bends the back,
making the skull beneath the skin
gleam like porcelain.

Seven years is a decent interval,
by any standard: widows remarry,
the roadside bouquets are long gone
at Millward's Corner.

Bandy-legged on the beach,
a bronzed octogenarian
swims to the buoy and back,
with the ease and grace of youth.

Anniversaries you should remember,
you forget, the ones you want to forget
you remember. This hot month
he would have been eighty.

Exeats

The red tail-lights would narrow, brightening
at the junction with the high road, then out of sight,
and we turned once more to the boarding-house.

Another wet weekend in Salisbury, Bournemouth
or Christchurch, our father catching up on British papers
or trying the patience of drunks – they only stopped him

for a bob, but his stories of an alcoholic father
and 'new starts' would leave their throats drier than ever.
At awkward and expensive mealtimes he advised us

about our 'hormones', whatever they were. Feelings
harboured for a girl glimpsed across the chapel,
were these the same chemicals in the blood that,

excepting exeats, had orphaned us? Praying myself to sleep
I dreamed god's house was a dormitory of girls,
though holding hands was banned, and praying together

the closest I would ever get to ecstasy.
Neither my father, his head buried in a book,
nor his surrogate in the skies, had much to say about that.

Winter Sunday evenings remind me of him;
I am wondering where he is on the London Road.
Clouds sweeping in from America rain on me.

Below Wytham

We moor in a crook of the Thames,
cross ancient meadows, skirting the fence
of the new research station,
and reach the metalled road to Wytham.

This way the ecologists would come
in their serious, shambling clothes,
on heavy black Humber bicycles,
or squeezed into the leather seats
of Professor Elton's Morris.

Which way into the wood? I point out
the passageways of voles and shrews
that are of no further human interest.
That mouse with the yellow ruff
has a tail that skins if held; it's only studied now
by the kestrel, hovering above us.

The flags have long gone, the strips of blue
or crimson cloth that showed where traps were laid;
he carried the aluminium boxes in a makeshift frame
that clanked upon his back; she followed with ribbons,
charting the route through the trees in a notebook
that's yellowed with age, and under the bunting
they spread their chequered rug.

Then Hamish, clad in corduroy and felt hat,
would stumble upon them, wielding a moth net.
"This place is like Piccadilly Circus," they'd groan,
hearing the Botany Section moving noisily towards them.

At dusk a mouse springs the trap under the last flag
shut; lights come on in 'The Wild Rose' –
tripping on tussocks, drenched with dew,
my boys come shrieking through the gloaming.
Tomorrow we go upstream to Lechlade.